Rock Solid Concrete Poems

Art Poems for the Heart

John Schmidt

Path Publishing

Amarillo, Texas

First edition

Path Publishing
4302 SW 51st #121
Amarillo, Texas 79109-6159
USA
Path@PathPublishing.com
PathPublishing.com

Cover by Path Publishing and CreateSpace
Poem on cover, "Fine Fat Cat," enclosed in this book

To order copies, see About the Author and the Publisher at the end of the book.

ISBN-13: 978-1500915926
ISBN-10: 1500915920

Printed in the United States of America

Dedication

For the eternal Spirit, from which all creativity bounds.

Contents

Acknowledgment

To my mother, who allowed me to experiment with hundreds of toys, including a chemistry set that smelled up the den, and in the early years taught me my letters and numbers.

Introduction

Art is for all of us. There is no obstacle to the understanding of oneself as long as one remains open to life and to art. If either of these doors is closed, the soul remains incomplete, far less than it could be. Meanwhile, the Spirit of the individual waits for something good to happen. Life should not be a waiting game, but should be embraced in all of its creative adventures.

These poems are but reflections of reality, yet like in the rest of life, great truth can be found in small things. Imagination makes the difference.

Imagination is an integral part of the human personality, and yes, soul. Once allowed to be developed, life and art and these poems can have greater meaning.

John Schmidt
April 19, 2014

I once
was filled with
myself like one of those
hot-air balloons lying flat on the
ground knowing nothing of its potential
to rise high in the clouds. Then I allowed
myself to be filled by an invisible force, my
Spirit, who was so much like the sky that
it took me with it. Now, as I soar above
all that was formally me, I forget the
level world of limitations and
breathe an infinity that
shapes a new world
in miniature.
At last,
I am.

Composition Squared

```
I once thought of being a great artist.
So                         proud.
I                             me
made            It          made
a             was  the      that
frame        mid-  dle      pine
of              that         ed
the            lacked      polish-
most        proper form.    was
beauti-                      it
ful                         and
 wood. Something to delight the eye;
```

We Attach Ourselves

we AttAch
ourselves to
these creatures   r
who know   o
   us better than we know ourselves. F
   in the petting of them we reach into
   an extended soul that unites us all in
   one blanket. Thus, we feed our own
   selves when we let the clamor of tiny
  c o flavor the unconditional lives o w
  h f   f e
  u m   w l
  n e   h o
  k a   o v
  s l   m e.

Sunrise Over Texas

When
I see the sun I sense
not only the heat that moves
my body from place to place but the
home of evolution, and once I am done
with my life below I may find a home for eternity. Let us not be surprised if there I never die.

Quite a contrast is my existence on an earth-based plain here
below where life and death are determined by the next breath,
and my days are as numbered. So I seek in this duality a calm
that unites fire and earth in one single thought within my brain.

Upon
viewing the
tree   of life
I wondered   why I
could   see
its   upper
part   but not
that   below.
Then I   looked
into   my own
soul and   saw
no roots   except
those planted by
parents,
society,
and a
foolish
self.
Thus I
can see
how trees
are watered
by rain and
I by tears.

Circle of Time

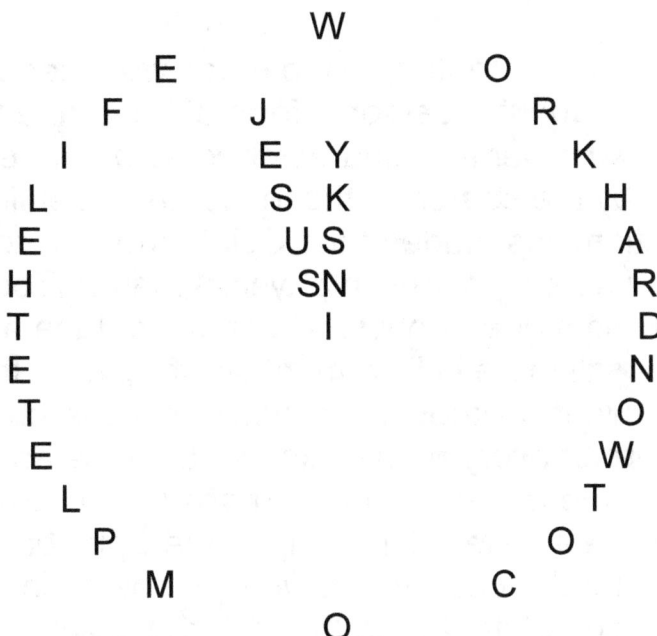

Topographical Search

Two
centuries ago much was made
about a person's form of head and face,
whether true character could be understood
by the search of those features. Yet little mention was made of the Spirit, and how to measure
its formulations in physical matter. Today, much
is made of physical beauty, of face and form—
still there is little mention of Spirit. If the truth
might be known, we would first search for the
core of every human and let the face and form
fall where they might. Perhaps in a thousand
years we will look upon the Spirit only,
for the beauty that we now see so incomplete. For in that day the Spirit
may be its own body, and move
about the universe as we
now turn pages in a book,
seeking the face to marry.

sit
with
me
and
tell
me
your
dreams,
and if you haven't one, that's
okay
,
you   don't
have   to
have   one
to   sit
with   me.

A rare bird

        can   birds

    who   fly   other   are

  bird   south   most   flying

a rare   when   north

         in the

         winter

Dedicated to Sandra Soli

I   would   rather
be   a sun-   filled
rose of light that
only angels see,
than a worldly
root
that
har-
bors
no
love
but
for
self
yet   has
the   earth
in   its
grip

I Am the Way

What does one do while walking on   w
a busy city street, totally preoccupied   r
by personal affairs, when suddenly one   o
notices that all the people are walking the   n
So does one return to one's roots, spirit-   g
ual or otherwise, or flow on silently to   w
an unnecessary mass destruction?   a
                                                    y
                                                    ?

Art Poem Can

Art
poem can only
be done when hands
of the clock signify there
is enough time. My life can
be best understood when
I put aside the clock,
letting poem be
me.

Fountain

every   fountain
  is first   a hidden
  pipeline   running
       under   the city
           with water from
           heaven

Big Shoes

My   Mommy
said I should put on my shoes and
tie them myself. Is she kidding? She
 knows I can't tie them myself. I wish I could
  but I always tie my finger in the string. I wish I
   had shoes like hers that just slip on. When I get to
   be big I'll   have shoes that don't tie.

Wrenching Happiness

                                                when
                                            a young
                    lad I was introduced to my father's tools, especially
                    his wrenches, for with them I could almost fix
          things.   But I never mastered them to more
                    than loosen the nuts on my bicycle. Then my
                    dad would patiently come along behind me and fix
                                            what I'd
                                            fixed.

Ants at a Glance

Ants   are   crazy
crea-   tures

    that   scurry   about   like
idiots   before   the   wind,

seem-   ingly   of   no
    great
  pur-   pose,   and

yet   there   must   be
  some   unity—   not

          as   scat- tered
as   it   seems
  on   the   sur- face—
        be-   cause
   they   tend   to   have
        only   one
       hole.

Red Wagon

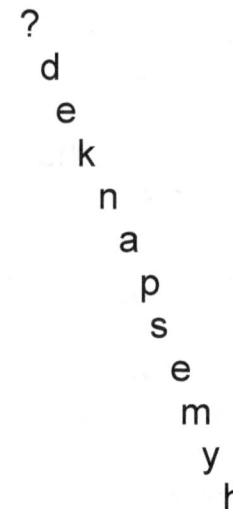

```
                                    ?
                                   d
                                  e
                                 k
                                n
                               a
                              p
                             s
                              e
                               m
                                y
                                 h
My red wagon takes me and Sally to the  w
next block where Mommy says we can't    o
ever go because we go cross the street.    S
      B                            t    to do it.
      u                            o
      t                            l
   I     S                      e     d
      a                            m
```

Red Wagon Revisited

My red wagon takes me and Sally to the
next block where Mommy says we can't
ever go because we go cross the street.
But Sal told me to do it.
So why me spanked?

On the Real Road to Myself

When I left home for the last time
(and there had been times before that)
my dad gave me $200 cash, a '58 Chevy
and a hug. I didn't see him again for years.
But the Chevy lasted for many years, as I explored the world, and myself, and as a young man became a real man. Or at least thought I was.

purrrrrrr!

```
I                                              ?
 t,                                          t
                                            a
    s            ay grand, is it          c
     I that ma      d      n      and I and
      o      k    r      o        t            !
      v        e  u      t   o        h        urrrrrrr
      e          s  o        ,   y        e        p     r
```

purrrrrrr! revisited

It's love that makes our day grand,
is it not, you and I and the cat?
purrrrrrrrr!

Let
me see
the face of
her yet to be.
Dare I imagine
one so distant
before I can
even hear
a word?
She is not so distant as I might
suppose, for in dreams, no one has

to be   filled out completely, least   not
the   girl of my dreams, who was   once
only   a dream. Yesterday, I think   I saw
her   but could not talk to her be-   cause
we   were both street strangers,   cut off
from   being more than walkers   by the
hurts   of millions, people who   took
not   a chance of talking to   one
who   might have been *the*   *one.*
But   now, I will never be   sure
be-   cause the chance of   love
         is replaced by silence
         and safety in numbers.

Western Friend

```
        that
  life is  which
  ner of   rivals dog
  man-       as man's
  what        best friend
  So            and serves
                to work long hours        without complaint
              and little compensation for its exertion except  b
              Or perhaps grass to long horizon. Very seldom  a
              do we consider how far back this creature's kin  g
              have served us. As we sit around the campfire   o
              telling stories of adventure and trial let us too    f
              marvel at our friends                    spe    f
                w  o                                   ak    e
                h  f                                   lo    e
                 o  n                                  u t   d
                 t  o                                  d h   ?
                 h  w                                  a  u
                 o  o                                  s  n
                 u  r                                  t  d
                 g  d                                  h  e
                 h  s                                  e  r.
```

22

Western Friend, Clarified

So what manner of life
 is that which
rivals dog as man's best friend
and serves to work long hours
without complaint
and little compensation for its exertion
except bag of feed?
Or perhaps grass to long horizon.
Very seldom do we consider
how far back this creature's kin
have served us.
As we sit around the campfire
telling stories of adventure and trial
let us too marvel at our friends who
though of no words
speak loud as the thunder.

Bart the Egg Man

Once an artist named Bart found himself in egg art—
boiled eggs with painted faces and heads,
dressed in coats and laces, with no legs.
When asked why he felt so free to
be an egg artist, he gave this list:
"Though some may say I'm cracked,
which makes me boil, I say I create
little people of distinction.
It began with Humpty Dumpty
Man in a vest, with a face where
shoulders should be.
But then came the rest,
little people of all
makes and descriptions.
See School Boy with red book,
and Banker Man with dollar signs
for ears, whose expression I took
from *Big Dollar* magazine.
This, Old Lace Lady,
sadness on her face,
for her son has just left, wedded—
and lonely she be.
These wee people, people me,
and to any who take time
to look, can see
some of themselves in the
egg-heads I paint."
A few of Bart's eggs
made it to an art show,
and wouldn't you know,
the curator was puzzled how to
show such delicate things—
especially Sleeping Man,
his eyes closed, who must
be lying on his side.
What could he say to Bart

if his egg-work was cracked
by some boy stepping back
into the lot, and eggs got knocked?
After several trials—
from egg holders to a Velcro bed
to adjustable arms holding up
each egg by three points—
a solution was found:
base of clay for the seven eggs—
especially molded for six egg bottoms
and one egg side—under a heavy,
clear plastic case, all atop
a pedestal of great weight.
Secure, yet efficient in cost,
smooth on one edge yet
ragged on the other side
to denote eggshells.
The eggs went to show,
but Bart did not know
if anyone liked his eggs.
To home and work he had to go.
The moral is (with no *eggaggeration*):
If you egg people on, they may think
you have fried all good taste, yet still delight in
your faces—which make them simmer in content.

Dedicated to Diana Ludwig, one of
my favorite people in all the world,
who, like Bart, exhibits dynamic
determination to reveal a marvelous
talent laced with sensitivity.

Experimental Spinach

This is
the worst stuff
in the world, thought
the child as he looked at the
mound of green stuff on his plate.
Until he ate. And rethought the lot: *Not bad,*
for scum. And Mommy said this comes before dessert.

       bird wings' whisper
     comes
to
   rest on
       snow—forest hears

Washington Visited

I
stopped
the tour
to spend
personal
time with
Washing-
ton at his
monument
and won-
dered, silly
as I be, if
he looked
down from
his height at
us, in tears.

```
Wine              glass
    crack         -ed
    new        light
       reflections
              e
              a
              s
              t
              of
            here
```

One Picture of God

```
              My
    neat.      teacher
    real         said
    was           she
    that         wanted
    thought       us to
    and          draw a
     of circles  picture
      a bunch  of God.
          I drew
                  My
        kids.   teacher,
       other      Ms. Keogh,
      like the        said
      and hands         that
      a face            God
       draw            is not
        me to        a circle.
          wanted   I think
              she
              I kept
          bushes. drawing
            and        circles
           trees         and
          drawed       circles.
           to me        She
             next       was
          The girl  not
              happy.
                    When
            fridge.  Ms. Keogh
             the            saw
            it to          hers,
            stuck           she
           Mommie           was
           home.            not
            my paper     happy.
             took       I kept
              and    drawing
             circles
```

30

Bookmark

The large book with an impressive
title was propped against the man-
tle above the fireplace, yet was not
ever opened except by a little boy
who out of curiosity wondered how
a book could collect so much dust.
Similar to the character of each of
those in the house, their ideals and
dreams not nearly so examined as
the morning newspaper. They lived
lives solitary and aloof from others,
died separately, and were seldom
remembered, even by the little boy,
who when a man, inherited the book
and house, soon sold both, moved
far enough away to ensure forgetful-
ness. Oddly enough, it was the book
that outlived them all, because I got
it at a library sale; it now resides on
my mantel, a silent reminder that I
should never forget to open myself.

Bush

Little
bush,   For
you   in
make   your
my   way
day. are
the
r
o of
o   t
t   i
s   m
e

Centered Thoughts

Centered
thoughts on peace,
Jesus,   make my
human   temple
a tab-   ernacle
to be   revered.
Even   when
I was   a child
I knew   this
but   was
not   recep-
tive   until
at   last,
an   older
man.

Plain Truth

It
was
Jesus
Who set the
plan before us when
He, there on the mountaintop,
refused to worship Satan and claim
to be a king on earth. Thus, we have inherited
the world, not by our righteousness, but by His humility.

Daisywheel

CONTINUOUSLYIDIEDUNTILILOOKEDATTHE

DAISYWHEELANDSAWIWASTHEHOLEINTHEMIDDLE UP

Daisywheel Clarified

Continuously I died
until I looked at the daisywheel
and saw I was the hole in the middle

        up

Sail Forth

Sail
forth on
the boat Mercy
and the first wave
back to your island
will be mercy
and the second love and the third
peace.

Worthy of Note

```
        t
       he
       mu  s
      e     i
      s     c
      s     i
      e     s
      n     t
      c     h
      e     e
      of    e
     what
  belongs most
  to me—my soul
 tuned by the song
    within God.
```

Dedicated to Jim Wilson, whose
humility rivals Paul McCartney

Bridge

I sit
on a high
rise above
a mountain stream,   a bridge
far away to my right.
The air is clear,
the sky bathed in sun,
and I jump hands outstretched,
hitting the two feet of water flat,   and death.
The mind is free to dissolve into the air it came from; the emotions
free to be water once again, the body back to earth in time;
spirit back to the sun from which it came. I
bounce back up from the water and sit again,
having visited eternity, thus infinite imagination.

```
            a life
     un-        folds
     like        an
     on-         ion;
     idea:          to
     find           the
      core       before
       you       die
            of

             t

             e

             a

             r

             s
```

train tracks are not for the weak hearted if you have

ever noticed they never give up until at destination.

Salesman

He
thrives
on it. Like
a mountain climber,
every moment the mountain
is rejecting him. At the top: he
may not be paid but in a long view.
But it's a view to last a lifetime—and beyond.

Let's Have Church

        t
     cross
        w
        n
      on
     the
   poorer
 side of town
 is a church
that's never
seen more
than a hundred
folks on any given
Sunday, and yet the
reign of God sits heavy
on the place and miracles
are as common as dust. Sister
Marcia, for example, has been healed
of about a dozen conditions in the last
40 years. Seven of her children saved
from temptation in a world full of it. No
one knows more   than she of the
grace of God.   She wants to
one day take   the message
of love to the   folks across
town, but we   all know they
are too chic   to fall for any
tricks, even   in His Name.

Doll

Most of
all she wanted
a doll to hold and kiss when
Mommy cried in the night for the
loss of her brother, when Daddy left
for work and never returned, when ZZ
the cat found a new home in the alley
with the other cats. Her doll would
never leave, no matter how dark
the darkness in her bedroom.
Years later, when she
graduated
from college,
she placed the doll next to her diploma.

Simple Cake

```
  I placed all around it, which is the  l
g                                        o
n  I wanted to bake a simple cake,       v
i  so at the top I placed a layer for    e
c  God and concerns of the world.        o
i  Below that, my family's needs.        f
e  Below that, the first layer I put     G
h  on the plate, self-concerns, the      o
T  foundation for the others above.      d.
```

Simple Cake, Revisited

I wanted to bake a simple cake,
so at the top I placed a layer for
God and concerns of the world.
Below that, my family's needs.
Below that, the first layer I put
on the plate, self-concerns, the
foundation for the others above.

The icing I placed all around it,
which is the love of God.

Close Reaching

No   together
matter   up—
how   taken
deep   and
a pit a   for
person   reached
can   be
fall   can
into,   who
there   her
is   or
always   him
      someone below

Telescopic Spirituality

When I was a child
I looked at the stars and the moon through
a telescope and mostly saw the world in black and white; but as
an adult, I turn the telescope to myself and see the colors of my
own aura, and I suppose, soul. These two
worlds, one glass.

To Moon and Back

I
was
looking
up at the
moon one
night and
wondered
if perhaps
I might go
there one
day via a
tall rocket,
that would
soar high
above all
clouds—I
would de-
scend to
a strange
new world
containing
marvelous
discoveries.
Perhaps I
would see
craters of
cheese or
a plain of
yogurt? I
dreamed
that night
of a visit
there and
instead, I
found my
God, Who,
smiling at
me, said,
"Look first
at space
in you, for
there you
will reach
mysteries
far greater
than cheese.

SIXTH STREET DINER

I'm not usually in the mood for a greasy hamburger but there is no other place open at this hour so a boxcar will have to do. I enter, wondering that the kitchen must be the smallest in the world. The waitress plops down a folded piece of paper, the menu. I speak the first items I see. I am content to be warm, hoping that a burger and fries will sustain my life one more day, one more dream.

Fine Fat Cat

```
        d                      l
      u   o                  l   h
    o       n              e       e
  Y        't            t           r
```

anything. You don't have to ask her
to sit still. She can park on the couch
for days and you can pass by and think
she has done nothing but breathe. Yet at
night you know she must have eaten some
grub and pooped. I do notice the increase
in smell when I pass the litter box on my
way to work. Otherwise I would never
know someone brought her to me
two years ago. Still, I'm glad
they did.

Dedicated to Karen Song,
founder of Li'l Orphan Nannies, a
company committed to saving the
lives of cats and dogs

Veggie Tales **Visited Firsthand**

           e
              h
Bob t to- mato
turned toward Larry,
who was, as usual, in his innocent
self, playing the fool, yet showing me a lesson
that any fool like myself needs to hear. I was eating
a sandwich. I noticed that the tomato juice was falling
on my clean pants. Did I care? Well, yes. But watching
Larry extricate himself from a predicament was far more
important than the fate of my pants, which I let go until
the end of the show and, I might add, the end of the
sandwich. What was the theme of the show? The
need to pay greater attention to life's small
joys and less to what people think.
This I accomplished.

Dedicated to the creators and
sustainers of *Veggie Tales*,
who feed us the fruit of wisdom

Hand of God in Man

God does not save us except

when we extend a hand to someone else, who perhaps

has never even thought of what it is to be loved—when we are

a friend, who may in the night only be able to give a hug

and say "I love you, and so does your Father."

About the Author and the Publisher

About John Schmidt

With forty years in creative writing, John Schmidt has published more than a dozen books, several e-books, a CD collection of many of his works, and a children's play—most through his publishing company, Path Publishing, and six through other companies. For more than twenty years he has been the editor of Path Publishing, releasing the works of twenty authors. Along the way he has earned Master's Degrees in English and Drama; spent several years teaching college and high school English; penned more than 2,600 poems; developed skills for writing in several genres, from nonfiction books to plays to poems to short stories; has given more than 285 free consultations to new writers; and has always encompassed a great love for creative expression and the human experience.

His Kindle eBooks, which can be purchased from Amazon.com, are:

Twelve Prose Works of John Schmidt, $9.99.

A Funny Thing Happened on My Way to the Muse—Humorous poetry and short prose to delight your life, $2.99.

And *Two Stories for Children—Betty Blooper Is Super! and Hands Holding Heaven*, $2.99.

From Smashwords.com, and its many apps, you can order *Forty Tips for Church Growth—A how-to guide for practical expansion*, $4.99.

The Collected Works of John Schmidt (Second Edition), a CD project in jewel case which can be used on almost any computer, can be purchased through PayPal at PathPublishing.com for $14.99 plus postage. More than a dozen of

John's works are in this 2,400 page collection, though it is without more recent works, *Rock Solid Concrete Poems*; *Heroes, Angels and Miracles*; *My Visit to the Kingdom of God*; and *My Return to the Future, 2350*.

To order a copy of *Rock Solid Concrete Poems*, purchase at Amazon.com or send $7.99 plus $3.50 shipping (with Texans adding 8.25 percent sales tax, for a total of $12.44) to Path Publishing, 4302 SW 51st #121, Amarillo, Texas 79109-6159.

All of John's works can be ordered through Path Publishing. For a complete list of releases, e-mail Path@PathPublishing.com. Postage is $3.50 for the first item and 75¢ for each additional. Or you can purchase most of his works through Amazon.com or the PayPal shopping cart at PathPublishing.com. Thank you!

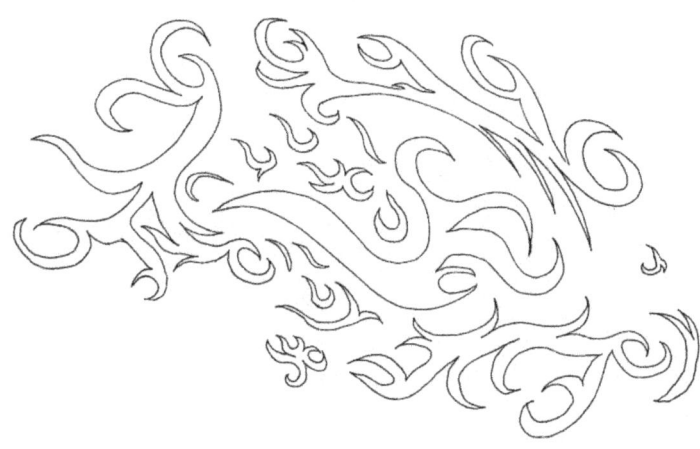

God's Breath, art by John Schmidt

About Path Publishing

Path Publishing began in 1993 and has published thirty-two books and other projects over the years, not counting e-books. We tend to specialize in general and Christian nonfiction, poetry, biographies, and self-help. Our website, PathPublishing.com, contains the works of many writers. In the past we have been listed in these publications: *Christian Writers' Market Guide*, *The Directory of Little Magazines and Small Presses*, and the September issue of *The Writer*, when they list publishers each year.

www.ingramcontent.com/pod-product-compliance
Lightning Source LLC
Chambersburg PA
CBHW081223170526
45165CB00009B/2932